Starting WeLL

A
DISCIPLESHIP JOURNAL
GUIDE TO HELPING OTHERS
Grow in christ

compiLed by adam R. HOLZ

NAVPRESS

Bringing Truth to Life

A *Discipleship Journal* Book
P.O. Box 35004, Colorado Springs, CO 80935
www.discipleshipjournal.com

OUR GUARANTEE TO YOU

We believe so strongly in the message of our books that we are making this quality guarantee to you. If for any reason you are disappointed with the content of this book, return the title page to us with your name and address and we will refund to you the list price of the book. To help us serve you better, please briefly describe why you were disappointed. Mail your refund request to: NavPress, P.O. Box 35002, Colorado Springs, CO 80935.

The Navigators is an international Christian organization. Our mission is to reach, disciple, and equip people to know Christ and to make Him known through successive generations. We envision multitudes of diverse people in the United States and every other nation who have a passionate love for Christ, live a lifestyle of sharing Christ's love, and multiply spiritual laborers among those without Christ.

NavPress is the publishing ministry of the Navigators. NavPress publications help believers learn biblical truth and apply what they learn to their lives and ministries. Our mission is to stimulate spiritual formation among our readers.

Discipleship Journal Books is a NavPress line of books on spiritual growth, produced by *Discipleship Journal* magazine.

CONTENTS

A LIFE WELL LIVED

Why discipling matters

by Sue Kline

SOMETIMES I FORGET WHAT COUNTS MOST IN LIFE. YESTERDAY WAS A
reminder.

Several hundred of us said good-bye to a dear friend. Jim had
finally been released from a body ravaged by cancer. Now we were
participating in a "celebration service"—a memorial to a life. Part of
that service included testimonies about how Jim had touched people
with grace.

A stream of men—young and not so young—came to the
microphone and talked about what Jim meant to them. "He taught
me how to memorize verses." "He played soccer with me." "He dis-
agreed with me—I wanted out of a bad marriage, and he had the
nerve to tell me it was the wrong thing to do." "His face always lit up
when he saw me." "He stayed later than anyone else to help clean
up." "He knew more of the Bible than anyone I ever met." "He didn't
just know Christ, he obeyed Him." "Even when he was too weak to
talk for more than a few minutes, he somehow managed to encourage me." "He had an uncanny ability to cut through all the layers and
get to the heart of a matter." "He was always thinking of ways to love

his wife more—and asking me to hold him accountable." "He loved me." "He was so honest about his weaknesses." "He was the most godly man I ever knew."

Jim was a husband, a father of five, a lover of Jesus, a friend to many . . . and a discipler of men. Midway through these overwhelming testimonies of a life well lived, I thought, *Yes! This is what it's all about. This is a man who never lost the vision for pouring his life into others for Jesus' sake.* I thought of the words of another discipler, words that Jim could have written himself: "We proclaim him, admonishing and teaching everyone with all wisdom, so that we may present everyone perfect in Christ. To this end I labor, struggling with all his energy, which so powerfully works in me" (Colossians 1:28-29).

Not long after surrendering his life to Christ, Jim claimed a verse of Scripture for his life: "Since you are precious and honored in my sight, and because I love you, I will give men in exchange for you, and people in exchange for your life" (Isaiah 43:4). The fulfillment of that promise was before me: men in their 50s, 40s, 30s, right down to rosy-cheeked young Air Force Academy cadets, all describing how Jim had discipled them. How he had stirred their love for Scripture. How he had stirred their love for the Savior.

A friend said to me as we left, "Jim makes me want to live differently."

Me too. In 1980, after nearly 30 years of self-centered living, I claimed that same verse in Isaiah 43. In its words I caught a glimpse of the breathtaking beauty of a life lived for eternity. My discipler wasn't named Jim—she was named Joyce. She loved Jesus, she loved God's Word, she loved people, and she wanted her life to count for the kingdom. Her zeal was contagious. I determined that I, too, would give my life to helping other people grow in the Lord.

I've never looked back, but sometimes I sure slow down. That's why Jim's memorial celebration moved me so deeply. I occasionally need to be reminded that few investments of my time and energy are as rich with value as the investment of helping another person grow in the faith.

And that's where this book comes in. Discipling a person one to one, life on life, requires heart, vision, and certain skills. *Starting Well* draws from some of the best material we've published in *Discipleship Journal* about helping young believers grow. In part one, we address the heart and vision of a discipler. We hope to help you see people with God's eyes and love them with the heart of Jesus. And we paint for you the big picture of what an hour or so a week can accomplish in another person's life . . . and in God's kingdom.

In part two, we get very practical, addressing many of the essentials that a just-starting-to-grow believer needs to know and do in order to keep going deeper in relationship with Christ. Your teachers in this journey are people who've devoted themselves to helping others walk faithfully with Christ. In a sense, this book allows them to disciple you as well. "Here's what new believers need to learn," they will tell you, "and here's how to teach it to them." That's as practical as it gets!

The Apostle John wrote late in his life, "I have no greater joy than to hear that my children are walking in the truth" (3 John 4). If you haven't experienced that sort of joy yet, then I hope this book will inspire you and equip you to plunge into the faith-building, mind-boggling, never-dull adventure of discipling another believer.

Sue Kline, Editor
Discipleship Journal

PART ONE

THE HEART
OF A DISCIPLER

CHAPTER ONE

THE ESSENTIAL INGREDIENT

Your heart to help someone grow

by Scott Morton

THIRTY YEARS AGO ON A BALMY OCTOBER AFTERNOON, A COLLEGE freshman sat alone in his dormitory, dreaming of a career in professional baseball—let's face it, he was a jock.

A knock on the door interrupted his reverie. There stood a tall, lanky student who introduced himself as Bob Van Zante. He was from the ballplayer's church, he explained, and wanted to welcome him to college and ask about his spiritual life. Cautiously, the ballplayer invited Bob in but was surprised when there was no hard push to get him to go to church.

Instead, Bob described his personal spiritual journey. Though religious, the ballplayer admitted he didn't know for certain if he had eternal life. Intrigued by Bob's genuineness, he agreed to join a weekly student Bible study, and though he wasn't faithful in attending, Bob stuck with him in the months that followed.

In April, the ballplayer quietly committed his life to Christ. A week later he was telling a dirty joke to some friends when an overwhelming sense of filth washed over him. "Guys, I can't finish this story," he said. "Something's different."

Bob continued to spend time with the ballplayer. They read the Bible together; they prayed together too. Bob helped the ballplayer memorize verses. They also had fun—together and with other believers Bob introduced to the ballplayer.

The ballplayer saw that Bob wasn't perfect: His social skills were awkward; he often put his foot in his mouth. But he was genuine. Once the ballplayer barged into Bob's room unannounced and found Bob on his knees in prayer.

Bob inconvenienced himself for that ballplayer and others in his study group. He was neither trained in theology nor gifted as a speaker, yet God used him to make an eternal difference: The ballplayer grew spiritually and started leading others to Christ.

Was it worth it? I think so. That ballplayer was me!

You Gotta Have Heart

If God can use Bob, he can use you to help one new believer grow. I can hear your objections: "I don't know my Bible well enough to help another person. I'd like to take a few Bible college courses first—and get my life more together. Give me a couple more years, then I'll be ready."

It's not what you know that matters. However little you may feel you know about the Christian life, you know more than a brand-new believer! What counts is your heart—and who resides there. Paul put it this way:

> When I came to you, brothers, I did not come with eloquence or superior wisdom as I proclaimed to you the testimony about God. For I resolved to know nothing while I was with you except Jesus Christ and him crucified. I came to you in weakness and fear, and with much trembling. My message and my preaching were not with wise and persuasive words, but with a demonstration of the Spirit's power, so that your faith might not rest on men's wisdom, but on God's power.
>
> —1 Cor. 2:1-5

Mighty Paul the apostle knew what it was to feel weak, inadequate, fearful. But he had the right heart—one filled with Christ. His first letter to the Thessalonians gives us a great glimpse of that heart—and a model to follow as we reach out to new believers and help them grow up in their faith in Christ.

An Interceding Heart

In 1 Thessalonians 1:2 Paul says, "We always thank God for all of you, mentioning you in our prayers."

Veteran Navigator missionary Warren Myers pointed out that much has been written about William Carey, the "father of modern missions," who served for decades in India 200 years ago, "but nothing has been written about his bedridden, 'useless' sister," who prayed for Carey and his converts hour after hour from her bed. That sister had the heart of a discipler.

When you pray for new believers, you are in good company. John 17 records Jesus Christ praying for His disciples. Colossians 4:12 describes Epaphras "always laboring earnestly for you in his prayers" (NASB). Note the words *always* and *laboring*. Not once in a while, but *always*. And *laboring*: Intercessory prayer is not dreamy reverie but hard work. Epaphras loved people enough to work hard in prayer. He had the heart of a discipler.

There is nothing better you can do for new believers than to pray for them. What can you pray? Scripture is rich with patterns for intercession—from Jesus' John 17 prayer to the many prayers of Paul that are recorded in his epistles. Read Paul's letters—especially Ephesians, Philippians, and Colossians—and underline or highlight in your Bible his prayers for fellow believers. In time, his prayers will become yours.

An Initiating Heart

Paul didn't wait for the new believers in Thessalonica to ask for help; he initiated help! Note 1 Thessalonians 2:2: "We dared to tell you his gospel in spite of strong opposition."

Parents don't wait for their new baby to invite them to "follow up" on the birth. Good parents take the baby home from the hospital to a room freshly painted and a little bed already made. Diapers, bottles, and burp cloths are neatly arranged. Parents take initiative.

Yet, with spiritual newborns, taking initiative requires taking risks. Your overtures to meet for Bible study could be rejected. You may feel as if you are crowding into their busy lives, inconveniencing them.

Jesus also crowded into a new believer's day. In John 9 He healed a blind man, who was then criticized by the Pharisees. They suspected a trick and even asked the man's parents if their son was truly born blind. Finally, they kicked him out of Judaism. Imagine the newly healed man's confusion!

Verse 35 says, "Jesus heard that they had thrown him out, and when he found him, he said, 'Do you believe in the Son of Man?'" Jesus took initiative to find the man and follow up on his new faith. He didn't wait for the man to find Him.

I'm glad Bob Van Zante took initiative to mentor me, or I would not have grown in Christ. I didn't even know which questions to ask! Think about it: Most of us, as new believers, did not seek out a Bible study or a mentoring relationship with a spiritual coach. Someone else dared to make the first move. A discipler's heart is a courageous one that takes the initiative in relationships.

A Motherly Heart

Paul says in 1 Thessalonians 2:7: "We were gentle among you, like a mother caring for her little children." Spiritual babies, like other newborns, need gentleness.

It was time for my regular meeting with Adam, an eager new follower of Christ. Boy, did I have a stiff spiritual pep talk ready for him! But as soon as we greeted each other, I knew something was wrong. So I spent the entire noon hour listening to him describe his new, hostile mother-in-law, who said to his new stepchildren, "You don't have to obey Adam; he's not your real father."

Adam was crushed. This was not the day for a pep talk. Rather, it was a day to be gentle. So I listened. Empathized. Part of the time we just sat in silence. Then it was time to go. As he opened his car door outside Taco John's, he paused, hugged me, and told me he loved me.

Gentleness means listening rather than fixing, keeping silent rather than speaking, putting an arm on the shoulder rather than an exhortation. Paul knew when to be gentle like a mother. Such is the heart of a discipler.

A Fatherly Heart

Not only was Paul as gentle as a nursing mother; he also played the role of the other parent by "exhorting and encouraging and imploring each one of you as a father would his own children" (1 Thessalonians 2:11, NASB).

At times you'll need to exhort a new believer to take a bold step for which he feels unprepared. Sometimes you'll need to do what it takes to prepare the person you're helping to make it without you — just as a father prepares his child for independence. Sometimes your fathering role will be to challenge another person to face up to a weakness or an obvious sin. It's daunting — and risky. But a father is willing to take the risk in order to see his children walk with maturity.

I once faced a "fathering" dilemma with Adam. He had a bad habit of rambling in conversation; his fiancée, Joan, had little chance to talk. He didn't realize that these rabbit-chasing, rambling soliloquies dishonored Joan.

I hesitated to exhort as a father for fear of losing Adam's friendship. Couldn't I, too, be accused of rambling?

Finally, during one of our biweekly get-togethers at Margo's Hot Dog Stand, I gathered up my courage and said, "Adam, as you prepare for marriage, I've got a suggestion." I told him courteously but frankly that he was violating a principle of good communication. And I gave examples of specific rabbits I'd seen him chase while Joan and others could only listen politely and check their watches.

Silence. *Uh-oh,* I thought, *he's not taking this very well.*

Finally, he smiled and thanked me. Then he asked how to overcome this bad habit.

At our next Bible study, he caught himself rambling, stopped, glanced at me, and smiled. Joan smiled, too, and started contributing.

That day at the hot dog stand, a victory was won—not just with Adam, but with me. God gave me grace to be more intent on pleasing Him than on pleasing Adam. God is the third party in a discipling relationship. He was present with Paul in Thessalonica; He was present with me at Margo's; and He will be present with you too. No one understands the father-heart of a discipler better than God.

Having the heart of a father doesn't always mean correcting. Sometimes it's a matter of encouraging or sharing a meaningful verse of Scripture. A good father considers the moment and asks, "What is most needed at this time?" A good father also realizes that children are different, and so he deals with them individually.

An Open Heart

Paul told the Thessalonians he was "delighted to share with [them] not only the gospel of God but our lives as well" (2:8). New believers need more than information or even inspiration: They need incarnation. They must see how the gospel works in everyday life. Words alone won't do it! How do you share your life with a new believer? Here are some suggestions.

Be vulnerable. Relate your struggles—not just your victories. People won't think less of you but rather will be encouraged that you are normal. I still recall the time I saw a mature mentor chicken out of a clear witnessing opportunity. He admitted it. Though he was discouraged, I was elated! I no longer felt alone in my struggles.

Get together. Notice the phrase "among you" in 1 Thessalonians 1:5 and 2:7. Invite your protégé to accompany you to the dry cleaners where you were bilked on a ketchup-stained jacket. She needs to see you struggle to be gracious and realize that she, too, needs to control her feelings and words. Let people you disciple see you live your life. Don't limit your contact to once-a-week, hour-long, structured appointments. **Open your home.** Bring them into your house or apartment. Let them see that your stove needs cleaning and your garage is a mess, lest they get the idea they must be perfect in everything. Let them observe your family relationships—how you have devotions as a family, how you handle conflict with a spouse or roommate, etc. They need to see that your relationship with Christ affects you on the home front.

All of this spells T-I-M-E. It's the most valuable thing you can give new believers. Bring them into your day-to-day victories and struggles. Anyone can share a message; it takes the heart of a disciple to share your personal life.

A Blameless Heart

Paul said the Thessalonians were witnesses as to how "holy, righteous and blameless we were among you who believed" (2:10).

One aspect of blamelessness is represented in the old saying "What you are speaks so loudly I can't hear what you say." There must be congruence between your message and your behavior. A friend once commented about a Christian leader, "I guess I respect him, but I don't want to become like him." Why not? Incongruence.

For example, you exhort your new believer to have a daily quiet time—do you? You extol the value of memorizing Scripture—do you? You frown at others who watch R-rated movies—do you?

It is hypocritical to lead where you are not modeling. Your protégé will see through it.

Paul mentions other areas that relate to blamelessness. In 1 Thessalonians 2:3, he assures his friends of the sincerity of his motives. In verse 5 he declares, "We never used flattery, nor did we put on a mask to cover up greed." In verses 4 and 6 he makes it clear that he is not seeking approval or praise from men; rather, he is seeking only to please God. Both Paul's motives and his methods were pure. His conduct was faultless. His discipler's heart was right with God and with man.

Walking Worthily

What goal did Paul have for the new converts in Thessalonica? What goal did Bob have for me, a baseball-crazed college student? Certainly, not all believers end up in vocational Christian ministry like I did. That's not the goal. Nor is it to make people better church members—though that happens. Rather, the goal of following up a new believer is that he or she "walk in a manner worthy of the God who calls you into His own kingdom and glory" (1 Thessalonians 2:12, *NASB*).

Paul wasn't content to *assume* the new believers were walking "in a manner worthy of . . . God." He knew they needed someone to be intentional about their growth. To the Corinthians Paul wrote, "Even though you have ten thousand guardians in Christ, you do not have many fathers, for in Christ Jesus I became your father through the gospel" (1 Corinthians 4:15). If everyone is responsible for helping new believers grow, then no one is responsible.

Has Paul's discipler heart stirred yours? Are you wondering where to start? Does a new believer's name come to mind? He may be flooded with Christian activities and may be busy in church, but he still needs a mentor, a loving friend to help him grow. Don't wait. Go to him and tell him you want to encourage him in his spiritual life. In that first meeting, tell about your spiritual journey and ask about his. See if God is leading you to meet again.

Can you do it? Yes! Allow God to stretch you. You can't go wrong following Paul's example in 1 Thessalonians. In the midst of many relationships, people need someone to take a genuine interest in them.

By the way . . . thanks, Bob.

Scott Morton is vice president of development with The Navigators and is involved in friendship evangelism, one-to-one and small-group discipling, and public speaking. He is the author of *Down-to-Earth Discipling* (NavPress).

CHAPTER TWO

"AM I YOUR PROJECT?"

Six ways to demonstrate genuine care

by Doug Wendel

"I FELT LIKE I WAS HER PROJECT," A DISGRUNTLED DISCIPLE CONFESSED to me. Her discipler, a good friend of mine, seemed sincere in her desire to help this young believer grow. I wondered what had happened.

In 1 Corinthians 3:9-10, the Apostle Paul referred to those he labored among as "God's building" and then called himself an "expert builder" in their lives. But how do we build into someone's life without making her feel like a project? Here are five practical ways we can communicate genuine love for those we are helping to grow in Christ.

Ask and listen.
Proverbs 18:13 tells us, "He who answers before listening—that is his folly and his shame." How can we truly help people without first knowing their needs? And how can we know their needs if we are doing all the talking?

The first thing we must do is to ask a few questions. I like to begin with some broad questions about a person's life. These create opportunities for him to share what he's thinking. Here are a few questions that may lead you into deeper conversations. Though they may seem basic, they demonstrate that we're concerned with all of someone's life, not just the "spiritual" aspects.

- How is your family doing?
- How are things going on the job?
- What has God been teaching you lately?
- How are you really doing?
- Are there particular areas in which you're struggling right now?

Then comes the hard part for some of us: sitting back and listening. Let them do the talking. Listen without making judgmental statements such as "You shouldn't do that," or "Do it this way." Ask clarifying questions if you need to, but give them your listening ear. Resist the urge to offer counsel or attempt to solve problems.

A few years ago I met regularly with a friend who had a hard time asking questions and listening. He tended to dominate conversations and jump very quickly from one topic to another. As we talked about his desire to help other men, he realized he needed to become a better listener. Today my friend is making a conscious effort to temper his talking by asking questions and listening, and he is becoming a more effective discipler.

If we don't ask questions and listen, we will be shallow disciplers. But when we do these two simple things, God opens doors to minister in deeper, more relevant ways.

Be flexible.

It's good to have a plan to help another person grow spiritually. But we need to remember that a plan is just that—a plan. Sometimes we have to put our plan aside to address matters of immediate importance in our friend's life.

Years ago a man named Jerry discipled me as a young Christian. One Saturday morning I walked into our weekly one-to-one meeting at Denny's restaurant feeling pretty low. Another young man I was discipling had criticized me that week for some of my failures. Jerry put aside his plans for that morning and listened attentively to my story. Then he affirmed me, saying I had done my best to be a good friend to the man I was discipling. Because of Jerry's flexibility, I walked out of that restaurant a wounded but healing soldier. His willingness to shelve his plan, to listen to my problem, and to encourage me helped me press on.

In discipling, we may create plans to help others grow. But we must never try to force people to conform to our goals at the expense of their hurts and questions. In short, a plan is made for the person, not a person for the plan. We must have the flexibility to let go of our agenda to address a pressing need in someone's life. This will breathe genuine love into our relationship with the person we are helping.

Be transparent.
Have you ever met a Christian who had it all together? I haven't either. Why, then, should we give the person we are helping the impression we are perfect? Even the Apostle Paul honestly wrote about his own struggle with sin: "What a wretched man I am! Who will rescue me from this body of death?" (Romans 7:24).

To help someone else walk with God, we must be transparent with our lives. This doesn't mean we reveal every detail. But it does mean we need to be honest about our struggles and failures. Being transparent accomplishes two things. First, it assures a young believer he is not alone in his struggle with sin. Second, it points him to Jesus Christ, the only one who can truly forgive and empower us to overcome our weaknesses.

Many of us have addictions we need to deal with. For some, it might be drugs, alcohol, or even food. For me, it's sports. The thrill of competition compels me to spend hours in front of the television watching athletes swat balls, shoot baskets, and bash bodies. One day I acknowledged my struggle to a man from church with whom I met regularly. After I finished talking, my friend looked me straight in the eyes. "I've got the same problem," he admitted. "And I don't want it anymore." We drew up a plan of action to work on our common struggle and decided to hold each other accountable.

Through our transparency, we empower those we're helping to be honest about their own struggles with sin.

Practice mutuality.

One misconception about discipling relationships is that the discipler does all the teaching and the disciple does all the learning. But someone with this top-down attitude will pour cold water into a relationship. Although one person may have more spiritual experience and maturity than the other, God wants both people to learn from one another. A sense of mutuality undergirds a healthy discipling relationship, a feeling that says, "We're in this together, learning from one another, spurring each other on in the Lord."

The Apostle Paul faithfully poured his life and teaching into many people, and he called them to follow his example. But he never set himself above them. In 1 Corinthians 11:1, Paul urged the Corinthian believers to "follow my example, as I follow the example of Christ." Rather than talking down to other believers, Paul called them to join him in his lifelong pursuit of Jesus.

Remember my friend who had a hard time listening? He was a wonderful encourager and faithful friend. Many times I left our lunch appointments energized by his friendship and sincere words of gratitude.

Through an attitude of mutuality in our discipling relationships, God will sharpen us and those we seek to help, just as Solomon described: "As iron sharpens iron, so one man sharpens another" (Proverbs 27:17).

Give grace.

When I was a college student, my small-group leader had a rule: If you came with your Bible study unfinished, you had to go to another room and complete it while the rest of the group participated in the discussion. During one particularly busy week, I arrived with my Bible study unfinished. I felt I was doing well just to be there. But my group leader thought differently. He refused to listen to my explanation and sent me out of the room feeling humiliated.

Looking back, I can see that my Bible study leader was trying to help me grow in faithfulness. But his "tough love" approach was not what I needed that morning. I had lacked time, not desire or discipline. What I really needed was an extension of grace that said, "You did your best. I understand."

In a discipling relationship, giving grace to others is vitally important. We all fail at some point and need to experience God's restorative touch through His people. When we extend grace to others, we emulate the Father, who "longs to be gracious to you; he rises to show you compassion" (Isaiah 30:18). We have all failed to meet His standard of perfection, yet He is so willing to forgive us.

God has showered each of us with abundant grace, mercy, and compassion. As disciplers, we should reflect the same mercy and grace. God is not standing over us with a big stick waiting to whack us when we make a mistake. Neither should we as disciplers be quick to correct those we disciple the moment they slip up. At times correction will be necessary. But any discipline should be cushioned by generous doses of God's grace and love.

The sum is love.

Treating each person we disciple with God's caring, tender love is the key to life-changing discipleship. By God's grace, those we're helping won't see themselves as our "projects" but as precious "buildings of God" being built for His glory.

DOUG WENDEL is a Navigator staff representative working with international students at the University of Oklahoma in Norman.

CHAPTER THREE

LOVE LESSONS

How to shepherd those we disciple as Jesus would

by Dirk Van Zuylen

"WHO HAS SIGNIFICANTLY INFLUENCED YOU?" THE SEMINAR LEADER asked. My mind began to scan the previous 32 years of my life. The first person who came to mind was my supervisor. Steve had shown confidence in me when I could only see my faults. Next I thought of Gordy, a man I had met in Holland in the '60s. He was a fun-loving, athletic friend. But more important, Gordy was in love with Jesus, and it showed in the Christlike way he related to people. As I reflected on what these influencers and others had in common, one thing came to mind: love.

The apostles had a lot to say about love. John wrote simply, "God is love" (1 John 4:8). Paul said unequivocally that "love builds up" (1 Corinthians 8:1). He also taught us that Jesus is the visible expression of God's love for us (Colossians 1:15-23). Following are some reflections on what we can learn from the life of Jesus about demonstrating love to our disciples.

Jesus showed confidence in His disciples.
Discipleship begins with a promise of life change. "Come follow

me," Jesus said, "and I will make you fishers of men" (Mark 1:17). Jesus promised that Simon, who had a very common name, would become Peter, the rock. Even though He predicted Peter's failure, Jesus could say, "When you have turned back, strengthen your brothers" (Luke 22:32). He had confidence in Peter's faith.

. The people who have loved me most have demonstrated confidence in me. My supervisor, Steve, had done exactly that in his previous professional evaluation of me.

I was leading a capable team of men and women at the time. Together, we shepherded a large and fruitful ministry. Yet even though God was obviously at work, I usually focused on my shortcomings. I remember saying to one of the men on our team, "You know, I'm never satisfied with anything I do." He replied, "How do you think that makes us feel?" I was always more aware of problems than of what God was doing among us.

Those feelings were foremost in my mind when Steve came for his regular "check-up" on our ministry. Despite my misgivings, he gave me a very positive assessment. At first I thought, *I wonder what he really thinks.* But his affirmation continued throughout the next couple of days. Finally, I began to get it: *He really does believe that God is blessing this work and that I'm doing a good job.* Steve's confidence in me gradually penetrated my tough skin.

We demonstrate love to our disciples when we voice our confidence in who they are and what God has called them to do. It's impossible to affirm people too much.

Jesus expressed His love for the disciples.

When bystanders saw Jesus' tears at the graveside of Lazarus, they observed, "See how he loved him" (John 11:36). Why did Jesus cry? After all, He was soon going to raise His friend; there was no need for such emotion. Yet Jesus cried. I believe He wept because His friend was dead and because He felt Mary and Martha's pain.

Unlike Jesus, I'm not naturally that demonstrative in my emotions. Over the years, however, I've worked on my ability to communicate love to those I influence. Sometimes that requires a physical or verbal expression of my affection. Other times, it might mean carving out time for someone when it's inconvenient.

Recently, a conversation with a friend encouraged me in this area. I was listening quite intently to this young mother as she described the complexities of her life. She was talking about the challenge of balancing her career and her family life when suddenly she burst into tears and ran from the room.

I was sure I had offended her somehow. In our next conversation, I tried to apologize. She stopped me and said, "No, it's nothing like that. When you were showing such interest in my life, it suddenly struck me how much I would have loved to talk these things over with my father. But he never seemed to have the time or inclination."

Showing love can be as simple as giving people a chance to share what's on their hearts. Ask God to show you how to let the person you're discipling know that you care.

Jesus demonstrated interest in the whole person.

Jesus showed genuine concern for those who followed Him. He provided not only for their spiritual needs, but for their physical needs as well. One example is when Jesus raised Jairus' daughter from the dead (Luke 8:40-56). Imagine if you or I had been at this amazing event. We would hardly have believed our eyes. We would have been dancing and hugging, probably laughing like people gone mad!

It would have been easy to forget the needs of the little girl whose life we were celebrating—which is exactly what happened. Suddenly Jesus told the onlookers to give her something to eat (verse 55). No one, not even her parents, had noticed that the little girl was hungry. Only Jesus had.

That story reminds me of a time when I spoke to a group of university students. After the message, I stood in back while everyone else enjoyed animated discussions. Nobody noticed me except one young woman. She asked if I would like a cup of coffee. "I would love one!" I said.

That young woman showed me love and encouraged me in a very practical way that day. We, too, can keep alert to simple ways to meet people's needs—whether those needs seem "spiritual" or not.

Jesus accepted people as they were.

I have often reflected on the variety of people Jesus attracted. He was a friend of social outcasts, and they invited Him to their homes for meals. He befriended the rich and poor, the healthy and sick, adults and children. They all wanted to be with Him.

That has not always been the case in my relationships. Once, a student I'd known for several years asked me if we could talk. When we got together, he read from a prepared text that listed some faults he had observed in my life. I will never forget one item on that list: "You reject those who don't agree with you." He was right, and I had to confess it. I had done a poor job of accepting people who were different from me.

The reason so many kinds of people were comfortable around Jesus was that He accepted them all. That didn't mean He wanted them to stay as they were: He protected the woman caught in adultery from a self-righteous mob of Pharisees, but He still commanded her to leave her life of sin behind (John 8:11).

In the same way, our love will be evident to our disciples when we accept them with kindness and grace in their areas of weakness (or in the ways they differ from us) even as we help them let go of sin. If we judge them harshly, however, we'll likely lose the privilege of speaking into their lives.

Jesus protected His disciples.

Every time the Pharisees attacked the disciples, Jesus came to their defense. Whether it had to do with washing hands, keeping the Sabbath, or tithing, Jesus was right there defending them. In John 17:12, He prayed, "While I was with them, I protected them and kept them safe by the name you gave me."

It was a sacred trust, and Jesus fulfilled it. He protected them by being with them and by praying for them. "I have prayed for you, that your faith may not fail," He said to Peter (Luke 22:32). Jesus didn't want His disciples to be isolated from the world, but He knew the world was a dangerous place. He protected them by teaching them to see the world from God's point of view. Jesus put it this way:

> My prayer is not that you take them out of the world but that you protect them from the evil one. . . . Sanctify them by the truth; your word is truth.　　　　　　　　　—John 17:15,17

We can demonstrate love for the people we disciple by protecting them as Jesus did: being with them, praying for their needs, and helping them understand how God's Word relates to their lives and struggles.

Jesus sacrificed for the disciples.

When Jesus finally laid down His life, it was the pinnacle of a life characterized by sacrifice. Jesus sacrificed heaven, with all its privileges and honor. He sacrificed earthly comforts, denying Himself sleep, privacy, and family life. His example is the one we follow:

> This is how we know what love is: Jesus Christ laid down his life for us. And we ought to lay down our lives for our brothers.　　　　　　　　　—1 John 3:16

When I was a young believer, I embarked on a rather unsuccessful campaign to avoid pain. But matters came to a head at a youth camp on the hills overlooking Beirut, Lebanon. I felt as if I wasn't giving everything to God. I reasoned with Him, "What more can I give? I've left home, I have no money, I've sacrificed my vocation. I've even left the love of my life to be here. What more do you want, God?"

"You've given me everything except your heart," I heard Him say gently.

I realized there was a connection between my love for Him and my willingness to sacrifice for others. As I looked over the sparkling lights of the city, this thought came to mind: *You die, or they die.* I needed to die to myself so that God could use me in a deeper, more lasting way to disciple others.

There was no choice really. He gave no less for me, because He loved me so deeply. May we do the same for the younger believers whose lives we touch as disciplers.

———————————————

Dirk Van Zuylen is a Navigator staff representative in England.

Chapter Four

WHAT MY DISCIPLER DID RIGHT

How an older woman helped my faith blossom

by Cathy Miller

THE MONTH I MET JESUS I ALSO FINISHED GRADUATE SCHOOL, DIS-covered I was pregnant with our first child, and moved with my husband to South America, where he was starting a new job. I was thrilled to be a Christian. But because of the crush of changes in my life, I didn't know that discipling was an option for new believers. I was too busy dealing with moving and morning sickness to do anything else.

When we arrived overseas, my longing for the familiar touches of American life drew me to a church in our neighborhood that held worship services in English. The expatriate community I met there was warm and welcoming, and it helped me adjust to life on foreign soil. Still, the idea of a discipling relationship never came up. The church focused on winning people to Christ, helping newcomers cope with culture shock, and serving others. While all of these things were important, my need was a bit more immediate: some good Christian friends to help me grow spiritually as I began to walk with Christ.

Three years and three countries later, a mature Christian woman approached me after a Bible study meeting. I had just expressed my opinion that Queen Esther was a manipulative woman, not to be admired at all. Looks of shock and disapproval flashed around the room. The women in the group avoided me as we filed out the door. All except Lorene. She walked beside me and gently touched my arm. "Would you like to come to my house sometime to talk?" she asked.

When we got together, I discovered that Lorene and her husband had moved to Latin America as missionaries after their children had grown and married. In the months that followed our first meeting, Lorene taught me the basics of the Christian faith. I don't think she used a specific *method* of discipleship. Rather, it was simply Lorene *being herself* that impacted me as she led me into a closer walk with Jesus. I was drawn to her unpretentious personal style and a life steeped in faith—a far cry from our self-conscious corporate lifestyle.

Not only did I grow in knowledge during our time together, but I found in Lorene's life a pattern to follow. Looking back, I can see that she exemplified several key traits that made her an effective discipler.

Availability

Lorene generously opened her schedule and home to me. Each time we met, I came away with books to read and Bible passages to ponder. It was then up to me to digest it all and call Lorene to set up a time to talk. We spent an afternoon together every week or two, relaxing on rattan chairs in her little upstairs apartment, frosty glasses of lemonade in hand.

"Jesus is always available for you," she taught me. "He's a gentleman. Spend time sitting with Him just like this, getting to know Him." The ceiling fan swirled overhead while we talked and prayed. I never felt like I was Lorene's discipleship project or a task to be completed. Her hospitality and willingness to meet made me feel valued and showed me that Jesus valued me too.

Flexibility

Like Jesus graciously feeding 5,000 unexpected lunch guests, Lorene always offered me a spiritual banquet. I don't ever remember a prepared lesson or an agenda for the day. Instead, our discussions were based on my questions, which were endless and pressing. I wanted to know about everything, and God blessed me with a friend who shared openly and freely. Lorene was remarkably "ready in season and out of season [to] convince, rebuke, exhort, with all long-suffering and teaching" (2 Timothy 4:2, *NKJV*). Her ability to teach in an unstructured way was especially helpful because we lived in a country where Bible study materials in English were difficult to get.

An Unflappable Spirit

On an intensity scale of 1 to 10, I was a 9 and Lorene was a 2. I zeroed in on every sticky theological question that came to mind. "Can you lose your salvation?" "What about the rapture?" "Why does God allow pain and suffering?" Lorene had dealt with these questions before, but she didn't respond with pat answers or memorized phrases. She let me wrestle with God's Word. Lorene encouraged me to search and struggle and come to terms with the questions of my heart. I could argue and probe and ask for 10 more verses to answer questions about each topic, but Lorene was never defensive or argumentative in return. She was steady, unhurried, unthreatened, and even seemed to enjoy watching God at work in me.

Careful Attention to God's Word

Every discussion we had was sprinkled with Lorene's favorite phrase, "The Bible teaches . . . ," followed by a truth or principle that would settle the point. She'd only let me go so far in my questioning; then she'd draw me back to the Word of God and have me underline and date a pertinent passage in my Bible. More than being mere words on a page, the Scriptures revealed a living God who was personally involved in my life.

I remember the day we looked at Colossians 1:27: "God has chosen to make known among the Gentiles the glorious riches of this mystery, which is Christ in you, the hope of glory." Lorene challenged me, "Meditate on this verse. It's the key to the Christian life."

I stuck little pieces of paper with "Christ in you, the hope of glory" on my bathroom mirror, the refrigerator, and the dashboard of my car. For weeks, our discussions centered around the mystery of grace and the indwelling Christ. I discovered life-changing truths in that passage as Lorene spurred me to think deeply about it. But she was always careful to give the Holy Spirit room to guide and teach me.

Creative Communication

Lorene filled our time together with creative illustrations and object lessons. Once I told her that my biggest fear was that God would make me move to some remote jungle as a missionary. She paused for a long time and then asked me to step over to her living-room window, which looked out on the Caribbean landscape.

"What do you see?"

"Nothing," I mused. "Just jungle."

"Now tell me how you've been spending your time here on the island." I could see that this was going somewhere, so I ran through my list of Christian activities. Teaching Sunday school. Hosting a women's Bible study. Providing housing for stranded Americans. Taking gifts to the leper colony.

"You *are* a missionary in the jungle," Lorene said, watching me. "So tell me, now that your worst fears have been realized, what else is keeping you from giving God complete control of your life?"

Lorene often used these kinds of concrete examples to help me understand and experience God in new ways. Another day, she placed a glass on the dining-room table and said, "When you first believed the good news of Jesus Christ and invited Him into your life, He came into your heart." She dropped a tea bag into the empty glass. Then she slipped away for a moment and came back with a steaming teakettle. The boiling water splashed into the glass and turned a golden color as the tea permeated it. "Being filled with the Holy Spirit releases the power of Christ in your life, making you more like Jesus." These were simple visual illustrations, but I still use them today as I teach others.

Encouragement

One time, I had an opportunity to take a turn teaching the women's Bible study Lorene and I attended. This was a first for me, and I prepared carefully, writing out everything I wanted to say. As I arrived at the study, I realized I had forgotten my notes! There wasn't time to drive back to my house to get them. So I took a deep breath, opened my Bible, and plunged into teaching. After the study, Lorene called and said, "God used you today to bless the women in our group." It was an encouragement I'll never forget.

Prayer

When Lorene and I met together, we always started and ended our sessions with prayer and frequently stopped during discussions to pray. "Pour out your heart to God," she urged me. "Learn to be real in prayer. God understands your emotions, your life. Come boldly, and be yourself. He can handle it, and you'll learn to trust Him along the way."

We prayed many different kinds of prayers: praising God without asking for anything; praying through lists of people who needed God's touch; asking for specific needs with deadlines; reading prayers from the Bible; even singing our prayers to God, making up the tunes and the words along the way. Prayer ushered me into God's presence, where I found that He Himself was the answer to my requests.

The Touch of Grace

What did my discipler do right? She noticed, cared, reached out, and pointed me toward the love of Christ as it is revealed in His Word and through His grace. Now, years later, I have opportunities of my own to pass on Lorene's legacy by quietly saying to someone else, "Would you like to come over to my house sometime to talk?"

CATHY MILLER is a freelance writer and conference speaker. She lives in San Diego with her husband. They have three gown children.

PART TWO

THE TOOLS OF A DISCIPLER

CHAPTER FIVE

FINDING THE RIGHT PERSON TO DISCIPLE

You want to help someone grow. But whom?

by Becky Brodin

"YOU KNOW WHAT, KATHY? I THINK YOU'RE READY TO DISCIPLE someone."

"Really?" She responded, blinking in surprise. "Do you think I could do it?"

I had been discipling Kathy for more than a year. She had a sensitive heart, a deep desire to know the Lord, and an eagerness to learn. I knew that if she could help a younger believer grow, her understanding of discipleship would soar.

Then she asked, "Whom should I disciple?"

That's a good question. A notice on a bulletin board at church probably won't work since many believers don't even know what discipleship is. I realized this a few years ago when I asked a woman in my Sunday school class to meet for coffee to talk about her spiritual growth. She looked at me like a deer staring into headlights, but she was willing, and we began to meet weekly. Several weeks later, she confessed she initially thought I wanted to scold her! She had been unfamiliar with one-to-one discipleship. Because many people we might want to disciple are similar, we will have to take the initiative to begin a discipling relationship.

For Kathy—and for us—finding someone to disciple requires three things: involvement with people, knowing what to look for, and a willingness to take initiative.

Pools of People

To find someone to disciple, you must be involved with people. In our culture, this is usually in the context of some kind of small group, such as a Bible study or a Sunday school class.

When Jesus selected His disciples, He did not run His finger down a list of names in the Galilee phone book and pick people at random. Luke 5 and 6 describe how He established Himself in the area. He preached, healed, ministered, and soon had a group of people following Him. Then, after a night of prayer, "he called his disciples to him and chose twelve of them, whom he also designated apostles" (Luke 6:13). Jesus was involved with people before He initiated with them individually. They knew Him, and He knew them.

Kathy participated regularly in a Sunday school class at her church and coled a small-group Bible study. I also knew she was actively building relationships. The stage was set for Kathy to look for someone to disciple.

The Right Stuff

What an interesting mix of men Jesus chose as His disciples! Laborers, political zealots, educated professionals. He looked past their personalities and professions for deeper qualities. While Kathy wasn't selecting apostles, she did need some criteria to help her evaluate the suitability of those she was considering.

Years ago a wise mentor told me to be patient with this step of the process. He suggested looking for someone who was hungry to grow and instructed me to wait and watch four to six months before I approached someone. When I asked him how I could tell, he assured me I would know.

He was right. Those who wanted to grow were committed to fellowship, studied on their own, and took the initiative to develop relationships. Though this list may seem subjective, it's a good place to start. It will help you identify those who are interested in spiritual growth and those who will follow through.

Kathy had been involved in her groups for several months. When I asked her who seemed spiritually hungry, she named two people: one from Sunday school and the other from her Bible study. She wanted to initiate with both of them immediately. But I convinced her to pray about it, following Jesus' example. After she'd done so, she was ready to take the next step.

Taking the Plunge

A discipling relationship is unique. It's personal. And it can be demanding, intense, time consuming, and life changing. Launching such a relationship requires initiative and honesty.

Luke 5:27-28 describes how Jesus recruited Matthew: "After this, Jesus went out and saw a tax collector by the name of Levi sitting at his tax booth. 'Follow me,' Jesus said to him, and Levi got up, left everything and followed him." The word *follower* in the Greek describes someone who seeks to be like his teacher, a companion who is "going in the same way." When Jesus called His disciples to follow Him, they knew what it meant. Whenever people chose to follow a particular teacher, they often left their jobs and current way of life to do so.

When Kathy and I talked about how to begin the relationship, I suggested that she clearly describe the discipleship process. What she was asking of these women would require a commitment of time and purpose. I urged Kathy to be honest about that commitment. Kathy and I had begun our relationship the same way.

On the Lookout

Kathy met with both people for more than two years. Then each of them began discipling others. But Kathy didn't stop there. She continues to watch for people who are hungry to grow, takes the initiative to relate to them, and invites them into a unique adventure of one-to-one discipleship.

―――――――――――――――

BECKY BRODIN is a Navigator staff representative in Minneapolis, Minnesota.

CHAPTER SIX

"LET ME ASSURE YOU . . ."

Discover the first five needs of every new believer

by Kathy Johnston

PEOPLE CONSTANTLY NEED ASSURANCE. WE DON'T LIKE THE UNCERtainty that comes with any new enterprise or relationship. That's why banks require collateral for their loans and employers check references before hiring.

Unlike certain bank customers and prospective employees, God is totally trustworthy. But a new believer who is taking those first steps of faith toward a God he doesn't yet know very well needs certain assurances. His mind whirls with questions: *Am I really saved? Will God keep His word? Will He hear—and answer—when I pray? Will He reject me if I sin? How can I know His will for me?*

When a mature believer comes alongside someone new in the faith and helps him solidify his sense of security in certain key areas, it whets the new Christian's appetite for intimacy with the living God, sparks his early growth, and gives him a foundation that will sustain him for the long haul.

What are the most important assurances for a new believer? The first step is always to make sure he understands the security of his salvation.

Assurance of Salvation

Many new believers have doubts about their salvation. The gospel seems too good to be true. Satan plants troubling thoughts: *Saying a little prayer to become a Christian was too easy. Surely I need to do more.* Emotions may shift: *God doesn't feel very close,* they'll think. This is why some people ask Jesus into their heart over and over again . . . just to make sure.

We must show those we disciple how the promises in Scripture clarify and affirm their identity as new creatures in Christ.

Recently I reviewed the gospel with a two-week-old Christian. Over lunch, I asked her, "Sarah, do you think you'll go to heaven when you die?"

"I don't know. I sure hope so."

"Did you ask Jesus into your heart?"

"Yeah, I did."

"Then let's read 1 John 5:11-12."

After fumbling to find the passage, she read, "And this is the testimony: God has given us eternal life, and this life is in his Son. He who has the Son has life; he who does not have the Son of God does not have life."

"It says here that you have eternal life in Jesus. But if that's not true, we might as well rip it out," I challenged her. The thought of ruining her new Bible got her attention. I went on, "Let me explain it this way." I picked up a cracker. "This is eternal life, OK?" I wrapped the cracker in a paper napkin: "The napkin represents Jesus." I handed it to her. "What do you have?"

Sarah paused, then answered, "Jesus."

"Right . . . what else?"

"Eternal life?"

"Exactly. Titus 1:2 says that God doesn't lie about His promise of eternal life. You asked Christ into your heart, and John 1:12 tells us you are part of God's family now. So if you were to die tonight, you'd be with Him in heaven. Does that make sense?"

"Yeah. It really does."

"Good . . . but since our feelings can sometimes make us forget what the Bible says, I brought some index cards. Let's look up some verses and write them on these cards. You can display them on your refrigerator as a reminder. Let's start with 1 John 5:11-12; then we'll look up John 1:12 and John 10:27-29. Then I think we should memorize the 1 John verses."

By examining the Bible's teaching about the security of her relationship with God, Sarah gained firm confidence in her salvation. Satan and her emotions would still whisper doubts in her ear from time to time, but she now knew where to turn for assurance.

Assurance of Answered Prayer

Once a new Christian is sure of his salvation, he's motivated to get to know this wonderful God. But baggage from the past may breed new doubts: *God's too busy to listen to my problems. If my dad didn't care, why should He?* or *Why bother to pray when God's going to do what He wants to anyway?* Meanwhile, the devil casts additional doubt on the goodness of God. So it's crucial for the new believer to know that when he cries out, his Father hears and cares.

A young Christian named Bill, entangled in adultery, told my husband about his affair during an early breakfast.

"It started out like any other friendship, Charlie. But it was wrong, I know. I've asked God to forgive me, but now what? I don't want to hurt my wife and son. I'm nervous because when I tell the woman it's over, who knows what she'll do!"

"Well, at least you've been smart enough to ask God's forgiveness," said Charlie. "And now you're ready to do the right thing and end the relationship. As for your fear of retaliation, remember, you've got a big God. In Philippians 4:6-7, God promises us His peace when we tell Him about our problems. Last week I was worried about coming up with money for taxes this year. Would you believe that the day after I prayed, a lady handed me a check saying, 'This is a refund from our taxes. God brought you to mind.' Jesus wants us to bring all our needs to Him. You need to give your fear of this woman to

God. I don't know how He's going to answer your prayer, but I know He'll listen because He cares about you."

They prayed, and Bill left for work. Later he phoned with good news. "Charlie, God really is looking out for me! The woman we talked about this morning called to say that she doesn't want to see me anymore. She's calling off the whole relationship!"

Bill learned a valuable lesson that day: When he prays, God responds. Hearing about one of Charlie's answered prayers planted the seed, but experiencing God's faithfulness firsthand cemented his assurance that God responds to his cries for help. In the days to come, Charlie showed Bill verses such as John 16:24 and Hebrews 4:14-16 to show him that our God truly wants us to talk to Him about everything.

Assurance of Victory

A new believer is easy prey for Satan, who will unleash an arsenal of temptations while whispering, "You may have resisted that last temptation, but you're way too weak to stand against this one!" That's why the person you're discipling needs the sure knowledge that he can survive temptations because God is faithful and can protect him.

Before Craig came to Christ, he had lived in the world of marijuana, materialism, and women. So the day he became a Christian, my husband read 1 Corinthians 10:13 to him: "No temptation has seized you except what is common to man."

Charlie then explained, "Basically, we all face the same stuff, Craig. You probably struggle with your thought life. I know how hard it is not to take that second look when I see a miniskirt. But there's hope for us. The verse in Corinthians goes on to say, 'God is faithful; he will not let you be tempted beyond what you can bear. But when you are tempted, he will also provide a way out so that you can stand up under it.'"

"How does He do that?" Craig wanted to know.

"I can't really answer that because it's different in every case. But I do know that whether you're fighting a desire for 'messing around' or for marijuana, God can help you."

Craig attended church with us the next day. Meeting other new Christians encouraged him; he saw he wasn't alone in his struggle to follow Christ. Later that afternoon he phoned.

"Charlie, thanks for inviting me to church. I'm glad I went. By the way, I told you I'd been heavy into drugs. But what I didn't tell you was that I grow my own plants in the basement—not to sell, just to support my own habit. Anyway, listen to this! When I came home today, I discovered that all four of my pot plants had died. I think God killed them."

After a moment of thought, Charlie replied, "Yeah, I think He probably did!"

Sometimes our Sovereign God works in unusual ways to rescue us. Craig experienced firsthand that His Father knows how much he can handle and will provide a way out. The next time Charlie met with Craig, they read the "Assurance of Victory" section in a little booklet called *Beginning with Christ* (NavPress), talked about temptations they struggled with, and thanked God for His faithfulness to them.

Assurance of Forgiveness

Satan knows that our growth ceases when sin cuts off our communion with God. That's why he feeds new believers lies such as, "You've really blown it now. God won't tolerate this kind of stuff!" or "You can't handle being a Christian, so why not go back to the old ways?"

It's our privilege to help young believers gain assurance of forgiveness—the joyful knowledge that when they confess their sin, God will cleanse them.

It's hard to be honest with others about our weaknesses. That's why we were surprised one night when, halfway through a couples' Bible study, Diane blurted out, "I've got a confession to make. I stole a tree from Wal-Mart."

"How do you steal a tree?" someone wondered aloud.

"Well, when I went through the check-out lane, I realized the total was low, but I didn't say anything. When I looked at the receipt at home, I saw they hadn't charged me for the tree. I still didn't do anything about it. That was two days ago, and now I'm really feeling awful."

"That's good," said Charlie. "God is convicting you, and you're responding. I'm glad you told us. Proverbs 28:13 says, 'He who conceals his sins does not prosper, but whoever confesses and renounces them finds mercy.'"

"That reminds me of 1 John 1:9," said Diane. "I read it this week. It says, 'If we confess our sins, he is faithful and just and will forgive us our sins and purify us from all unrighteousness.'"

Charlie probed, "Is that something you want to do tonight, Diane?"

As we prayed with her, Diane experienced God's peace. But she still looked puzzled. "What should I do now? I can't take the tree back. I already planted it!"

"What do you think you should do?" I asked.

"I've got a pretty good idea . . . but it won't be easy."

Diane and her husband left early that evening, heading north toward Wal-Mart.

Two days later, we did a Bible study about forgiveness, using a book called *Lessons on Assurance* (NavPress). We were both encouraged by Psalm 103:12: "As far as the east is from the west, so far has he removed our transgressions from us."

That passage affirmed what God had already done in her heart. Diane now had assurance of forgiveness.

Assurance of Guidance

Giving your life to Christ implies giving God control. That's scary for a new Christian. He may wonder, *Can God really lead me? Will He ask me to do something I don't want to do?* The enemy's intention is to thwart the potential service of the young believer. So it's crucial to strengthen his conviction that even though he may not have a clue about what lies ahead, God's plans for him can be trusted.

Sue and I had just finished a quiet time together when she said, "Kathy, sometimes I wonder what God can possibly do with me. I've got so much to deal with from my past. Can He still use me?"

"You'd better believe it. God's got something good in mind. In Jeremiah 29:11 He says, 'For I know the plans I have for you . . . plans to prosper you and not to harm you, plans to give you hope and a future.'"

"You know, I sense that," Sue responded. "In fact, it seems impossible right now, but I feel like God wants me to be a missionary someday. How can I really know His will for me?"

"Look up Proverbs 3:5-6," I told her.

She read aloud, "Trust in the Lord with all your heart and lean not on your own understanding; in all your ways acknowledge him, and he will make your paths straight."

"You don't have to know all that lies ahead, Sue. Just keep trusting God and talking to Him, and He'll lead you day by day. Let's pray about it right now."

After I opened in prayer, Sue shared her heart: "Lord, You've been giving me a lot of wisdom since I've been reading Your Book. It's about time for me to give back, so if there's someone who's needing what I've got, show me what to do."

Before we parted that day, we read about some men and women in the Bible who needed God's guidance. David prayed to understand God's will before going into battle. Daniel asked the Lord for help to interpret Nebuchadnezzar's dream. Esther needed courage and wisdom for presenting the plight of the Jews to the king. After seeing God's faithfulness to direct each of these people, Sue could hardly wait to see how He was going to lead her.

Three days later she phoned me. A friend who'd "hit the wall" had just called her. Sue told him all that Jesus had done for her, then she connected him with her pastor. God's guidance in answer to Sue's sincere prayer made her day . . . and mine!

Deep Roots

The heart of follow-up is life on life, not mechanically covering content. Yet understanding these basic needs of a new convert provides a blueprint. As you've seen, there are many ways to strengthen a young believer's security—including memorizing verses, exploring what the Bible says on a topic, relating stories of how God has worked in your life, and looking at biblical examples. Once a new Christian is assured of the steadfastness of God's promises in the foundational areas of salvation, answered prayer, victory over sin, forgiveness, and guidance, he is ready to "continue to live in [Christ], rooted and built up in him, strengthened in the faith, . . . and overflowing with thankfulness" (Colossians 2:6-7).

Kathy Johnston and her husband, Charlie, are on staff with The Navigators in Nebraska. Kathy is a retreat speaker, Bible study leader, discipler, and freelance writer.

CHAPTER SEVEN

QUIET TIME BASICS

How to help a spiritual neophyte spend time alone with God

by Mike Hildebrand

BOB MAGNUSON WAS ONE OF MY FIRST SPIRITUAL MENTORS. HE AND his wife, Judy, had discovered the secret to a powerful, effective ministry to young college men: food. Every Thursday evening I joined them for the best spaghetti and cinnamon rolls on the planet. But it was the feast after dinner that filled my real hunger.

Each week, Bob and I would read and discuss the Bible. Bob's favorite quote from Jesus was from John 6:63: "The words I have spoken to you are spirit and they are life." The Scriptures always came alive when Bob talked about them.

Bob helped me begin to develop my own relationship with God. He understood that the substance of Jesus' ministry to His disciples was to pass on to them His relationship with His heavenly Father. In the same way, Bob brought me into God's presence. He let me in on the intimacy he had with his Savior, and I began to learn what it meant to know and love God. Bob modeled what it looked like to relate closely to God and taught me how to sustain that relationship through a daily quiet time.

Helping another person become more intimate with God is an

essential goal of discipleship. Teaching that person how to have a quiet time on his own is one practical way to accomplish this goal. What follows is a simple guide to that process.

Showing Them Why

The purpose of spending time alone with God daily is to develop intimacy with Him and to learn how He wants us to live. When I begin to teach someone about a personal quiet time, I believe it's important to help him see the biblical basis for this practice. To accomplish that, I ask him to consider what the following passages say about the value of spending time with God regularly.

Ex. 33:11	Ps. 73:25-28	Mt. 11:28-30
Ps. 5:1-3	Ps. 143:8	Mk. 1:35
Ps. 16:11	Jer. 2:32	Lk. 10:38-42
Ps. 27:4	Mt. 4:4	Heb. 4:14-15

After he's had a week or two to take a look at these scriptures, we discuss the following questions:

- What is a quiet time?
- How often would it be good for me to spend time alone with God?
- When during the day did people spend time with God?
- What might be my purpose when I have a quiet time?
- What is God's desire when I meet with Him?
- What might I hope to gain by having quiet times regularly?

This exercise helps establish the conviction that having a quiet time daily is a practice God's Word describes and endorses.

Showing Them How

After we've established the biblical basis for quiet time, I like to show him how to do it. So we have a quiet time together.

Psalms is an excellent book to help a young believer begin to relate intimately and personally to God. I usually select a psalm that corresponds to the day of the month or one that is related to an issue the person is facing. We read the entire psalm together and then go back and alternate reading one or two verses at a time. As we do so, we respond to God by praying those verses back to Him. The intent is to interact with what God is saying in the verse in a way that connects it to our lives.

For example, if I read "The Lord is my shepherd, I shall not be in want" (Psalms 23:1), I might pray, "Lord, thank You for taking care of my needs." Because I am almost always anxious about something, I mention that specific concern in my prayer and state my trust in God to take care of it. Make sure to pray about the things that are important and personal to you, just as you would if you were having a quiet time alone with God. Then let your friend have a turn, and pay attention to what he prays.

Using Psalms in this way creates plenty of opportunities for vulnerability before God about the issues of day-to-day life. I have to be prepared to confess sin, to acknowledge my weaknesses, and to throw myself on God's grace and mercy.

Engaging the Scriptures

In addition to helping people relate intimately with God, we want to teach them some basic questions to ask about the scriptures they read. I use a simple acronym called PEA to introduce a three-step process of mining truth from God's Word: *Principle, Example, Application.* In most of the scriptures they read, people should be able to identify each of these three elements.

Let's look at how this process functions by using a familiar story: Mary's and Martha's interaction with Jesus as recorded in Luke 10:38-42.

As Jesus and his disciples were on their way, he came to a village where a woman named Martha opened her home to him. She had a sister called Mary, who sat at the Lord's feet listening to what he said. But Martha was distracted by all the preparations that had to be made. She came to him and asked, "Lord, don't you care that my sister has left me to do the work by myself? Tell her to help me!"

"Martha, Martha," the Lord answered, "you are worried and upset about many things, but only one thing is needed. Mary has chosen what is better, and it will not be taken away from her."

Principle. I ask the person I'm helping to consider this question: *What principle(s) do I see in this passage?* He might respond, "The main thing I need to do as a follower of Jesus is to sit at His feet and listen to His Word."

Example. The next question I ask him to think about is, *What examples in the lives of people in this passage should I imitate or avoid?* He might answer, "I need to imitate Mary's willingness to listen to Jesus instead of being distracted by urgent but less important tasks."

Application. Finally I ask him to consider, *How can I apply to my life what I've seen in this passage?* He might conclude, "I need to pay more attention to the things that stress me out and keep me from spending time alone with God."

Getting Them Started

Sometimes, even after I teach someone how to have a quiet time on his own, he may struggle to integrate this habit into his life. A few years ago, I met every Friday to have quiet times with a friend. Once I asked him how his quiet times were going during the rest of the week. I was jolted to learn that he'd never had one except when we met. I had shown him how, but I'd never gotten him started on his own.

The next week I came to his house on Wednesday morning. We selected a passage and sat at opposite ends of the patio, where he had his quiet time alone and I had mine. That step may seem simple, but it was something my friend needed to help him discover he could spend time with God without me directing each step.

Pressing On Together

One thing I like best about teaching others how to be intimate with God is that it helps me keep that focus myself. I love to pray that prayer of Jesus: "I have made you known to them, and will continue to make you known in order that the love you have for me may be in them" (John 17:26).

_____

MIKE HILDEBRAND is a former Navigator staff representative who has a ministry with businessmen in Phoenix, Arizona. He is currently a financial consultant with Smith Barney.

CHAPTER EIGHT

LEARNING TO TALK

How to use the Scriptures to launch a young believer into prayer

by Lee Brase

EVERY GROWING BABY NEEDS TO LEARN TO TALK IN ORDER TO NAVIgate his new world. Likewise, learning to pray—that is, talking to God—is a foundational building block in every believer's relationship with God.

We might think that learning to pray happens naturally. For some people, prayer may in fact come easily. But we shouldn't assume that someone we're discipling intuitively knows how to talk to God. After all, even the disciples were unsure how they should pray. Like little children, they said to Jesus, "Lord, teach us to pray" (Luke 11:1).

Prayer is learned the same way a child learns to talk. First, a child listens to others. Then he imitates something he's heard. Children learn to speak by mimicking words and sounds, not by formal instruction.

Jesus knew that the disciples would need words to "mimic" if they were going to speak the language of prayer. So He said, "When you pray, say . . ." (Luke 11:2). He taught them to pray by giving them a prayer. Samuel Chadwick understood this when he wrote, "The only way to learn to pray is to pray."

Over the years, I've had the privilege of helping many young believers learn the language of prayer. The most effective way I have found to do this is to take them to the prayers in the Bible.

A Prayer for All Seasons

I find that God has recorded prayers in Scripture for every occasion: for praise, thanks, grief, pain, frustration, warfare, joy, and more. Just as Jesus offered His disciples a model prayer, so the Scriptures are full of prayers we can use to help a young believer learn to talk to the Father.

If someone is burdened by excessive stress, for example, I might take him to one of David's prayers, such as Psalm 57 or 63. Both of these psalms were written while David was running from Saul. Or if someone has a wayward child, we might look at Exodus 32 to see how Moses prayed as he led his rebellious people. If someone wants to pray for the ongoing spiritual needs of others, I might show him the prayer of Jesus in John 17 or the Apostle Paul's intercession in Ephesians 1.

Keeping in mind that prayer is a language, I begin by trying to help people imitate the words of Moses or David, Paul or Jesus. Next, we work on putting these prayers into their own words, for their specific situation.

For example, when David was fleeing from Saul, he prayed, "I am in the midst of lions; I lie among ravenous beasts—men whose teeth are spears and arrows, whose tongues are sharp swords" (Psalm 57:4). These words perfectly describe what David was facing. But the person I'm mentoring faces his own unique struggles and battles. To put the prayer in his own words, I would encourage him to pray something like this: "Father, I am in the midst of a lot of uncertainty and stress. I feel as if my life is being drained out of me." It's important that people who are learning to pray be very specific with God about what they are experiencing.

Through the Eyes of Prayer

The next step is to help people observe the heart and vision of the person whose prayer is recorded in the Bible. I do this by asking several questions.

1. **What were the circumstances surrounding the prayer?** What caused the person to cry out to God?

2. **What did the person believe about God?** What titles did he use for God? What kind of attitude did he display toward Him? What did he recall about God?

These are critical questions because our concept of God will determine how we talk to Him; it determines what we can believe Him for. In the Lord's Prayer, Jesus believed that God was the heavenly Father. This concept of God spurred Jesus to ask for the Father's will to be done on earth as it is in heaven. It also caused Jesus to believe that the loving Father would give His children food, forgiveness, and protection.

Someone who is learning to pray needs continual encouragement to grow in his understanding of God. For novices in prayer, the study of God Himself is more important than the study of other prayer topics, such as spiritual warfare, which can be covered as his prayer life matures.

3. **What is the major content of the prayer?** What did the person praying spend most of his time talking to God about?

It still amazes me how different the prayers in the Bible are from most prayers today. The praying people of the Bible took time to review who God was and what He had done in the past. Many of the prayers in the Bible contain several verses but have only one or two requests. When the early disciples' lives were threatened, for example, their prayer began by focusing on how God had ruled in sovereignty throughout history. They ended by asking for boldness, that God's power would be demonstrated (Acts 4:24-30). It is essential to take beginners in prayer to passages such as that one. That's how they learn to pray about what's on God's heart rather than praying selfishly.

4. **What, if anything, did the person ask God to do?** It can be surprising to see what someone in the Scriptures requested in light of his apparent needs.

5. **What did the person who was praying expect to see changed as the result of this prayer?** This question is closely related to the

preceding one. It's valuable to check Scripture to see how God answered a particular prayer.

6. If you are looking at an Old Testament prayer, how might that person have prayed in light of the death and resurrection of Christ? As a general rule, New Testament prayers are primarily concerned with the inner life of God's people, not with the destruction of an enemy or physical needs. For instance, David often asked God to destroy his enemies. When Jesus came, however, He told us to pray *for* our enemies, not against them (Matthew 5:44).

In the Old Testament, the blessings of God on His people were usually directed toward the fruitfulness of their land. This was because God's people lived in one location: Israel. The fruitfulness of their land was a sign to other nations that the God of Israel was blessing them. In the New Testament, God's people are scattered throughout the world. His blessing has to do with fruitfulness in their lives (John 15).

Discipling others in prayer goes well beyond helping them learn to pray for a given situation. The goal is to help them become attentive to God and to grow into people who long to communicate openly and to live in utter dependence upon Him. When these things happen, prayer becomes the rich, organic language it's meant to be.

LEE BRASE is the international prayer-ministry coordinator for The Navigators. Lee is also the coauthor of *Praying from God's Heart* (NavPress).

CHAPTER NINE

OUTREACH 101

First steps into the world of evangelism

by Evan R. Griffin

"HOW DO I TELL MY FRIENDS ABOUT MY RELATIONSHIP WITH JESUS without scaring them off?" Steve asked. As one of my graduate teaching assistants, Steve had been watching me and asking spiritual questions. The week before he informed me that he had invited Jesus to take over his life. Now he wanted to know how to begin sharing this new life with his friends.

Here are four steps I use to help young believers such as Steve communicate the good news in winsome, relational ways.

Help them remember.

The first step is to help your young friend recall the changes Jesus brought about in his life. When he remembers what life was like before Jesus entered the picture, it will help him identify with the lost in his world.

Action Step: Have your spiritual apprentice write down all the ways his life has changed since Jesus "moved into the neighborhood" (John 1:14, *The Message*). These could include changes in thinking, feelings, motivations, values, behaviors, goals, and relationships.

I recently asked a new believer I'm mentoring, "Brad, how did your life look before you started following Jesus?" He responded, "Life just wasn't working. I felt the classic hole inside. Each new distraction worked for a while, but soon the novelty evaporated, and my awareness of how empty I was returned. It wasn't pretty." When I suggested that maybe some of Brad's friends could identify with that feeling, I could see the light bulb come on in his mind.

Help them research.

Study God's Word together. Certain Scriptures can help a young believer begin to feel what the Lord feels for the lost. For instance, at a recent retreat I facilitated a discussion of Matthew 9:35-38 with a group of college students. Several were captivated by verse 36: "When he *saw* the crowds, [Jesus] had compassion on them, because they were harassed and helpless, like sheep without a shepherd" (emphasis mine). The students asked God to help them begin to see the lost with compassionate eyes, as He does.

Action Step: Read the following passages together and discuss the questions that follow.

- Matthew 9:35-38: How might it feel to be a shepherd who cares about harassed and helpless sheep?
- Luke 15: How do you think you'd respond if you lost something of great value and then found it again?
- Jeremiah 2:13,25; John 4:1-54, 7:37-39: How would you respond to thirsty people trying to find their own water instead of receiving the free, clean water you offer?

Research their world together. In Acts 17, Paul walked around and took note of all the idols in Athens. He then shaped his message to that context and even quoted one of their own poets. An equivalent today might be drawing a principle from a hit movie, television show, or song. In other words, we want to help a young believer become a "pedestrian anthropologist," someone who understands the people to whom God has called him to minister.

Action Step: Take a "prayer walk" together around his school, workplace, or neighborhood. Ask God to do the following:

- break up the hardened soil of people's hearts (Hosea 10:12)
- develop spiritual thirst in them (Psalm 42:1-2)
- help them see how He is working (2 Kings 6:17)
- prepare you to share your faith (1 Peter 3:15)
- help you listen patiently and carefully (Proverbs 18:13)
- help you speak wisely and graciously (Colossians 4:5-6)
- draw your friends to Him (John 6:44)

Help them relax.

Many young believers mistakenly believe that outreach means backing up the "gospel dump truck" and burying someone in a pile of theological truth. But we don't have to accomplish everything in one conversation. Reaching others with the gospel is a process. Sometimes it goes quickly, but more often the process is gradual.

When a young believer understands this, it can take off the pressure and help him to relax. If he can see that his job is simply helping someone take the next step toward Christ, he will be less intimidated.

When Tony and I began meeting, he was convinced he was "the poster child for introverts." He didn't think he would be able to witness to others. Since then, however, he has taken the risk of saying hello to some of his classmates. He's introduced himself and begun to ask friendly, nonthreatening questions that demonstrate his interest in their lives. We have celebrated these first steps together.

Action Steps: Here are some simple activities to help a young believer initiate relationships with lost people. Encourage him to try a couple of these ideas this week.

- Say hi when you see your nonbelieving friends. Be friendly, joke around, and have fun with them.
- Say affirming, encouraging things.
- Offer to help them accomplish some task: raking leaves, shoveling snow, moving furniture, and so on.

- Invite them to join you in your everyday activities such as eating, shopping, seeing a movie, or running an errand.
- Make them cookies or brownies.
- Ask them to help you with something.

Help them relate.

The last step is to help your friend begin to relate spiritual truth to the lives of his lost friends. To do this, he needs to see what it looks like to embrace others in love while simultaneously exposing them to truth. We need to look for opportunities for our friend to see this in action.

In his first week as a new believer, Steve watched me interact with one of our students who was having an "emotional meltdown" after class. She felt overwhelmed by her friends' relational demands on her. I listened, empathized, and comforted her. I finished by making a simple observation about how much we desperately want people to be strong enough for us in a way that only God can be. When Steve and I talked about the experience afterward, he commented, "Evan, I think I could do that."

Action Steps: Two easy ways to enable a young believer to engage meaningfully with the lost are asking questions and telling stories. Jesus often used both in His teaching.

Questions. Asking questions gives us an opportunity to understand what life looks like from someone else's point of view. I've encouraged Steve to invite one of his lost friends out for a cup of coffee, ask him how he's doing, and *really* listen. It's important to emphasize that the purpose of questions is not to create a "set-up" to pounce on people with our spiritual claws out. Rather, it's to draw them out and give them an opportunity to share their lives.

Here are several questions I've used; I encourage those I'm mentoring to give them a try.

- What makes you feel that life really matters? What gets you out of bed in the morning?
- How do you feel your life is working these days?

- When do you feel the happiest? The saddest? The angriest?
- Whom do you look up to and respect? Why?
- What's your religious or spiritual background, if any?
- When has your spiritual interest been the strongest? The weakest? Where do you feel it is now?
- If you wanted to grow spiritually, how would you go about it?
- What do you think about Jesus? Have you ever read the stories about Him for yourself? Would you have any interest in that?

Stories. Some people will argue about theology, but it's hard to argue with someone's story, such as the tale of the blind man in John 9. As we help our apprentice tell bits and pieces of his spiritual autobiography, the potential for meaningful conversations increases dramatically. Help him brainstorm some interesting stories he can tell his friends. For example:

- humorous preChristian experiences with churches, Christians, etc. These stories help lost people know we can identify with them.
- exciting "new believer" stories about our experiences with church, the Bible, worship, life changes, etc.
- answers to our prayers
- bite-sized stories of how we were drawn to Jesus
- meaningful fellowship stories, such as the way a friendship developed on a retreat, in a meeting, in a small group, in a Sunday school class, etc.

One of the most appealing aspects of Christianity is the relational depth and camaraderie that can result when people have Christ in common. Others will be drawn to it. My younger brother, now a children's pastor, admitted that he was initially attracted to Christ because of my friendships with other believers.

If we can help our spiritual apprentices focus on these four areas, we'll launch them into a lifetime of outreach.

EVAN R. GRIFFIN is adjunct professor of communication at the University of Cincinnati and a Navigator staff representative at the University of Cincinnati and Xavier University.

CHAPTER TEN

CONTAGIOUS LOVE

Passing on your passion for God

by Cindi McMenamin

"CAN WE MEET SOMETIME AND TALK?" HEATHER ASKED AS I WAS packing up my teaching materials after the Bible study.

"Sure! How about now?" I responded. We ended up at a local coffee shop where Heather asked a slew of questions.

"I'm trying to learn all I can about walking with God," she said. "What books would you suggest that I read?"

I rattled off the titles of a few classics while Heather took notes.

"What else do you think I should be doing to grow spiritually?" she asked next, posing the question every discipler longs to hear.

I mentioned a Sunday morning class I would soon be teaching and a discipleship group being offered that summer. I could tell by the look on her face, however, that my answers weren't what she was hoping for.

She dropped her eyes, and I sensed a bit of hesitation. "I want to, umm, be able to know the Bible and talk about it like you do."

"Oh, so you'd like to teach?"

"No. I just want to, you know, get excited about it . . . really *live* it."

Suddenly, I understood.

Heather wasn't looking for books to read or things to do or classes to take. She didn't want to know more. She wanted passion. She was searching for something to engage her heart.

Our conversation opened my eyes to an element of discipling I hadn't considered. It's fairly simple to communicate a list of things to do and beliefs to understand. But how do we pass on our love for God?

I went home that day and began to take inventory: What had helped me move from knowing *about* God to a loving relationship *with* Him? As I began to share the following ideas with Heather, I watched her transform from a woman who simply professed Christ into a passionate follower.

Express your commitment daily.

Three basic principles have helped deepen my relationship with Jesus. They're easy to remember and can be done every day. When Heather began to practice them, she found they made a world of difference in her love for God.

Tell God first. When I have exciting news, when my world crashes in, when I'm facing something bigger than I expected, I tell God about it before I tell anyone else. Sure, He already knows. But by going to God first with the things that are closest to my heart, I reaffirm to Him and to myself that He is the most important person in my life.

Take God seriously. I've found that I need to know what God wants from me and make His will a priority. I take God seriously when I find out what He loves and cling to it, and when I become aware of what He hates and avoid it at all costs. I explained to Heather that taking God seriously means I prioritize my life so that nothing steals time from nurturing my relationship with Him.

Trust God fully. Sometimes God asks something of me, or allows something to happen, that I don't understand. That's where trust comes in. Trusting Him fully means I take my greatest fears to Him and place them at His feet. Heather and I talked about how to acknowledge that God is in control of our lives and how to trust Him to shape us for His purposes (Romans 8:28). For example, when I say to God daily, "No matter what comes my way today, nothing comes between You and me," I am cementing my love relationship with Him.

Look for God all around you.

After Heather joined my Jazzercise class, we explored how each workout could be an expression of praise to God for the bodies and health He has given us. She began to see that worship could be incorporated into every facet of her life. Bringing God to our Jazzercise class brought up the question of how to look for Him (and how to praise Him) everywhere we go and in everything we do.

I told Heather about the day I took my daughter, Dana, to see *Hercules*. Although the movie is based on Greek mythology, one scene paralleled what Jesus did for us. After Hercules died to rescue the woman he loved, he became immortal. "Dana," I whispered excitedly, "that's what Jesus did for us—He gave His life for us so that we won't have to die. Now He lives eternally, and so will we!" The illustration made a lasting impression on my six-year-old daughter; the next day I heard her tell a four-year-old friend the story of salvation.

We can find God and examples of His story anywhere: in the beauty of creation, in the lyrics of a song, in a movie scene, in an exercise class. As I showed Heather how to be alert to God in everyday life, her relationship with Him began to encompass everything she did, not just church and Bible study.

Linger in God's presence.

The next time Heather and I got together, I told her what makes me want to meet with God every day. She was interested to hear that I originally set a daily appointment with God out of obligation. But after discovering some meaningful ways to get into His Word and to worship Him, I began coming to Him because I wanted to. The more I lingered with Him, the more my love grew. I suggested that Heather incorporate the following elements into a regular time with God.

Spend time in Psalms. Because these emotional songs engage our hearts, it's difficult to encounter them without being changed by their passion. Together, we paraphrased a psalm, personalized it, and prayed it back to God. We even sang one. Heather was excited to realize that some of the songs we sing in church come straight from Scripture.

Put yourself in the picture. I showed Heather how to read one of the stories in the gospels and put herself in the place of one of the characters. How would it feel to be talking to Jesus face-to-face? What would He tell her? What might He be saying to her now about a personal situation? As Heather began to experience Jesus as a person, not just a belief, reading the Bible became something she looked forward to.

How can you pass along *your* love for God to the person you're discipling? The ideas I shared with Heather were meaningful to her because they came out of my personal pursuit of God. The ways you maintain a love relationship with God will likely be different from mine. But no matter how we express our love for God, Heather's questions helped me understand how important it is that the relationship shows. When our passion for God is visible, the person we're discipling may be prompted to ask, "How can I experience that too?"

CINDI MCMENAMIN is a pastor's wife, Bible teacher, and speaker from San Marcos, California.

CHAPTER ELEVEN

SCRATCHING WHERE THEY ITCH

Discerning your disciple's needs

by Mistie Hutchison

"I LOVE DISCIPLING YOUNGER WOMEN," MY FRIEND COMMENTED, "but I'm not always sure what I should do with them!"

I can relate. I thoroughly enjoy the opportunity to walk alongside someone and see her grow as a follower of Jesus. But sometimes figuring out what to do next is tricky.

It's not that I don't have plenty of resources. I have a file on most aspects of the Christian life that I can readily turn to for ideas. No, the hard part is determining what the person I'm helping really needs. As the old saying goes, you have to "scratch where they itch."

So how do we determine someone's needs in a discipling relationship? Here are some ideas that have helped me.

Ask God for guidance.

Asking God for discernment sounds almost too obvious, doesn't it? Yet I've noticed in my own ministry that it's easy to forget to ask for God's direction; instead, I can subtly slide into relying on my own experience and knowledge. After meeting with someone I'm discipling, I often catch myself running through a list of things to do when we meet again: a passage to study, an article to read, or a point I want to talk about.

Because of this tendency, I've asked the Lord to alert me when I begin to make plans without seeking Him first. I want to discern what God might want to accomplish in a person's life and to cooperate with Him in this process. He often reveals needs I wouldn't see.

I'm convinced this is one reason Jesus spent so much time in prayer. Before major decisions (such as choosing His disciples, Luke 6:12-16) or key times of revealing Himself to others (such as when He walked on water, Matthew 14:22-33), Jesus prayed.

Listen attentively.

A while back, I was talking with a friend of mine about her relationship with her supervisor. She said, "My manager may not always agree with what I think we should do in a given situation. But that's OK, because I know he really hears me when I talk." Her comments reminded me of the importance of listening carefully to others as we seek to discern their needs.

It's one thing to remember what we've been told, to make eye contact, and to say "uh huh" and "I see" at appropriate times. Effective listening, however, goes beyond the right techniques; it means actually *hearing* the other person, entering into her life and seeing the world through her eyes. It means embracing her thoughts and emotions.

If we hope to serve the real needs of those we disciple, we need to know what's going on inside them. They will be much more willing to talk about the deep things of their hearts when they sense that we're listening carefully.

Ask good questions.

To listen well, we need to ask good questions. Broad questions can help us discern needs at the beginning of a discipling relationship. I've found the following questions helpful:

- What do you feel your needs are?
- How can I help you?
- Where would you like to see growth in your life?

As we get to know a person better, our questions will become more focused as specific issues emerge.

I recently asked a woman I've begun discipling what she thought her needs were and how I could help her. She was unsure how to answer. Though she described a desire for personal development, she wasn't clear what that would look like. I asked a few more questions in an attempt to stimulate her thinking, but we didn't get much farther.

Our conversation showed me that this woman needs to get to know herself better. By asking questions and listening carefully, I was able to identify a concrete area in which I can help her.

Differentiate between felt needs and real needs.
When we ask someone what her needs are, we may discover that her perspective is different from ours. Paul found this to be true in his relationship with the Corinthians. He wrote, "I gave you milk, not solid food, for you were not yet ready for it. Indeed, you are still not ready" (1 Corinthians 3:2). The Corinthians seemed to think they were more mature than they actually were. Paul saw that they still needed to be grounded in the basics of following Christ.

We, too, may need to help someone grow in an area she has not identified on her own. For example, I once discipled a young woman named Brenda who thought her most important need was learning how to be a godly wife and mother. This is a noble aspiration, and I wanted to encourage her in this desire. However, Brenda wasn't married, didn't have any children, and wasn't dating anyone.

In this situation, Brenda was articulating a *felt need*. Felt needs are those things a person thinks are most important. They often arise out of a specific circumstance, or out of our desires or our sense of missing something in life. Brenda's legitimate desire to be a good wife and mother was a felt need that occupied her thoughts and emotions.

After I spent some time asking questions and listening to Brenda, I began to see a greater need in her life, something I refer to as a *real need*. Real needs are the things that God is orchestrating in our lives to take us to the next step of maturity. They relate to core beliefs and values we hold about ourselves, others, and God.

God helped me see that Brenda believed her performance (that is, being prepared) determined what He would give her and when. Her real need was to come face-to-face with her desires and God's sovereign goodness in her life. As our relationship grew, I was able to share some of my observations about this deeper need in her life.

In discipling situations where felt and real needs seem to collide, the issue isn't deciding which is "right." Both are legitimate. Rather, the issue is discerning what God is doing in a person's life and helping her see Him at work. Often, as was the case with Brenda, someone's felt needs can serve as a bridge to addressing the real needs.

Moving Forward

The process of discerning someone's needs doesn't have to be a game of hit-and-miss. If we're willing to seek God, listen carefully, and ask good questions, we'll be in a much better position to identify a person's real needs and to decide what to do next. Perhaps what she needs most is practical help getting into Scripture. Or maybe she just needs someone who'll listen to her story for a while before "doing" anything.

This process may involve extra time and effort, and it does force us to relinquish our agendas. But the rewards of being in step with God's work in another's life are well worth it.

MISTIE HUTCHISON serves on the leadership team of The Navigators' EDGE Corps, a short-term ministry-training experience for recent college graduates.

CHAPTER TWELVE

FOUR WAYS TO DO ONE-TO-ONE

There are more ways to disciple than you might realize

by Joan Esherick

WHEN I FIRST WENT TO COLLEGE, I ASSUMED EVERYONE'S CHILD-hoods were similar to mine. Surely everyone knew how to swim and paddle a canoe; surely everyone had hand-milked a cow.

How surprised I was to discover that it wasn't so! I felt both foolish and thankful: foolish at my naive presumption, thankful for my experience.

I felt the same after becoming a Christian. I assumed most new believers met with an older, wiser Christian to learn about following Jesus. After all, that was what I had done for four years. But when my husband and I moved to Philadelphia so he could attend seminary, I again discovered that I was mistaken. Even seminary students didn't have what I'd been given! That's when I realized discipling was a gift I needed to give to others.

In the 20 years since, God has given me the opportunity to disciple many new and not-so-new believers with varying needs and availability. Each relationship has had its own character, joys, and challenges, but all have testified to what God can do when one believer invests in another.

What follows are case studies of those relationships. Some describe a single discipling experience almost exactly as it happened; others represent a composite of several relationships. (Names have been changed and details altered to protect the privacy of those involved.) I hope this glimpse into the experience of one imperfect, yet willing, discipler offers you a wider view of the ways discipling can be done.

Case Study One

Liz: "I want to know more about my faith."
Method used: STUDY
Meeting type: Weekly 90-minute sessions
Meeting place: My dorm room or hers
Duration: 15 weeks (one semester)

Liz, a new believer and fellow college student, was the first woman I discipled. I had only been a believer for three years, but our campus ministry leaders thought I could help her with beginning questions. We designed our meetings around Liz's desire to learn more about basic Christianity. Though we sometimes touched on personal issues, we focused on a set curriculum. We used what I now call the STUDY method of discipling.

Set a weekly meeting time and an end date. Liz and I agreed to meet every Tuesday evening. To solidify our commitment, we set an ending date before we started (which also provided a clear way to finish if the relationship didn't work).

Talk to God at the beginning and end of each meeting. Because Liz was unfamiliar with—and initially uncomfortable about—praying aloud, I modeled prayer by opening and closing our first few sessions with a simple petition for God to be with us, teach us, and help us apply what we learned. As the semester progressed, I introduced Liz to word prayers and sentence prayers. Eventually my lone prayers of less than a minute gave way to 10-minute conversational prayers that bracketed our study.

Use curriculum. Because Liz hungered for foundational knowledge, we used the first three books of the *Design for Discipleship* series (NavPress), one of many excellent discipleship tools available today. Each week we both completed one chapter of the study guide, which we discussed later along with any additional questions Liz had.

Do your own homework. In addition to the week's chapter, I prepared for questions that might arise and provided historical background, biblical context, or cultural information that would help Liz. Though I tried to be thorough, I couldn't know everything; sometimes Liz asked questions I couldn't answer. I didn't hesitate to say, "I don't know, but I'll try to find out."

Yield the results to God. Though I gave Liz biblical facts and doctrinal truth, I couldn't impact her heart; only God could mold and change her. I found great freedom and patience as I entrusted the results to Him.

My positive, though imperfect, experience with Liz set the stage for other one-to-one relationships. While Liz broadened her foundation, I learned discipling skills and gained confidence in God's ability to use me.

Case Study Two

Sharon: "I'm grounded in the faith, but I want more depth."
Method used: GROW
Meeting type: Biweekly two-hour studies, monthly special outings, and a miniretreat
Meeting place: A small, private room at church for study; other locations varied
Duration: One academic year, September to June

My investment in Sharon, an acquaintance from church, began when she asked me to disciple her. She wanted to deepen her walk with God, so we met twice a month to examine Bible-study methods and spiritual disciplines. Unlike Liz, Sharon didn't want to use a structured study guide. Instead we used a hodgepodge of Scripture and classic books such as Ole Hallesby's *Prayer*, Richard Foster's *Celebration of Discipline*, A. W. Tozer's *The Pursuit of God*, and Brother Lawrence's *The Practice of the Presence of God*. We learned to GROW together.

Guide your disciple to the tools and disciplines necessary for growth. Even though Sharon knew the basics, she didn't know about Bible-study methods, concordances, topical Bibles, commentaries, Bible dictionaries, and Christian classics. We spent our first week going over study tools, methods, and books that would enhance her personal study and then used them throughout our time together.

Sharon, however, needed more than books and study skills: She needed to experience Christ's presence. To help foster that awareness, we chose a "discipline of the week" (such as silence, solitude, meditation, worship, listening, surrender, or service) and practiced that discipline until our next meeting. Our nine months together culminated in a miniretreat (six hours one Saturday at a vacationing friend's empty home) where we could practice our newly learned disciplines with minimal distraction.

Release your disciplee to grapple with God. I was tempted to respond to Sharon's every question with concise, tidy answers. In order to grow, however, she needed to wrestle with some questions on her own. Rather than defining surrender, for example, I asked Sharon what she thought it meant. I then encouraged her to do a biblical word study of *surrender* (including *submit, yield, give*, and *offer*). At our next meeting we discussed her discoveries. As Sharon sought answers from God (apart from me), her connection with Him grew.

Offer practical tips. I encouraged Sharon to write Scripture verses on index cards and to leave them where she'd see them. I taught her how to give her thoughts to God. I showed her how to pause for "meditation moments" throughout her day (for example, when the clock chimed, she could reflect on an attribute of God). I called attention to the ring I wear to remind me of God and gave her a similar ring when we parted ways. Sharon longed to know God's presence but often forgot He was there. She simply needed practical ways to remember Him.

Weave spiritual discussions into everyday life. In addition to our regular study times, each month Sharon and I spent an afternoon together. One month we took a hike to enjoy and worship God. Another month we attended a concert and discussed Christ, the arts, and what it means to honor Him with our entertainment choices. Several times we met just for coffee or breakfast. By spending recreational time together, we were able to discuss everyday challenges and broaden our sense of God's involvement in our world.

Helping Sharon discover a deeper relationship with God filled me with joy. I would have been delighted to keep meeting, but by the end of the year Sharon outgrew what I could give. She continued to walk deeply with God on her own.

Case Study Three

Tina: "I need an older, wiser friend to model a life lived by faith."
Method used: WALK
Meeting type: Informal and irregular, but frequent
Meeting place: My home, her home, walking trails, coffee shops, the car
Duration: Long-term, open-ended (ours lasted until Tina moved away)

Tina, a young believer from a broken home, needed someone she could observe and learn from in ordinary life. I mentored Tina by learning to WALK with her.

Welcome your disciplee into your life and home. We invited Tina over for dinner now and then; she also joined me on errands or stopped by just to hang out while I did daily tasks. This life-on-life discipleship required availability. Though I didn't plan it, our deepest discussions occurred in unexpected moments that would never have happened in a structured study.

Accept help from your disciple. Tina occasionally took my kids (all three of them, at her initiative and expense) to the movies, park, or ice cream shop so I could rest or study. My children relished these outings as much as I treasured the breaks.

Tina also helped with house projects, which gave us time to discuss whatever was on her mind. Allowing Tina to serve us gave her more time to talk and let her see how our functional, though imperfect, Christian family applied biblical truth to everyday life.

Let your disciple see your flaws. Tina watched me obey Christ *and* fail Him. My very human mistakes revealed my need for Jesus and dependence on Him. When I allowed Tina to glimpse my struggles, she saw how I learned to trust God in adversity, how I surrendered unanswered questions to Him, and how I repented when I sinned. For example, when I told her that I lost my temper with my eight-year-old son and had to ask for forgiveness from God *and* from my son, Tina learned how conflict can be reconciled and result in growth.

Know when to say "when." Sharing life with Tina was a privilege, but I also needed to guard my heart, my family, and my privacy. Because Tina knew she was welcomed and loved, I could say, "This afternoon won't work. Can you come over next week?" Setting boundaries modeled the way to establish and follow priorities—something Tina might not otherwise see.

Though Tina would say she received the most from our friendship, her generous spirit and desire to know God refreshed and encouraged me. I felt like Tina gave far more to me than I gave to her.

Case Study Four

Natalie: "I'm in crisis!"
Method used: HELP
Meeting type: Telephone calls and informal get-togethers
Meeting place: Natalie's home, restaurants, and walking trails
Duration: Short-term crisis intervention until we found a good support group

When my neighbor Natalie's husband died, she faced a crisis unlike any she'd ever known. Though we weren't close friends, Natalie respected my faith and asked if we could talk. I fumbled my way through our initial discussion but eventually learned to HELP.

Hold hands. While many others offered practical assistance, Natalie needed me to walk with her through her crisis of faith, to be someone with whom she could weep and process her questions. Sometimes she cried, while I said nothing. At other times, I assured her that her confusion and anger were normal responses to loss. I actively listened, sat with her, and prayed.

Encourage with truth, not platitudes. Natalie was receptive to God's Word once she knew I wouldn't minimize her pain. I reminded her of God's faithfulness and sovereignty and that we can trust God with our heartbreak and confusion. Though grieving, Natalie embraced God's comfort and peace.

Lead them to the proper support channels. I provided biblical encouragement and appropriate resources (C. S. Lewis' *A Grief Observed*, for example), but Natalie needed to connect with others in similar circumstances. I found a local grief support group and offered to attend the first meeting with her. Though reluctant, she agreed and then began going on her own. This group of grieving women offered support and understanding I couldn't give.

Pull back when other support systems are in place. Natalie needed my involvement in those first weeks. But as time passed, others were better suited to meet her needs. We stopped meeting two months after her husband died. I often felt inadequate, but I considered my time with Natalie a privilege because she allowed me to walk with her in suffering.

Liz, Sharon, Tina, and Natalie: four lives, four seasons, four sets of needs. Yet God used our relationships to teach us more about Himself and to make us more like Jesus. I am a better discipler—and disciple—because of each one.

JOAN ESHERICK is a teacher, discipler, and speaker from Telford, Pennsylvania. She is author of *Our Mighty Fortress: Finding Refuge in God* (Moody).

DISCIPLESHIP ILLUSTRATIONS: THE WHEEL AND THE HAND

The Wheel Illustration

DAWSON TROTMAN, FOUNDER OF THE NAVIGATORS, LOVED USING concrete objects to illustrate spiritual principles. One such illustration has become known as The Wheel and depicts the Christ-centered life of a disciple of Jesus. It is an excellent tool for ensuring that you and those you are helping are moving toward a balanced and vital life with the Lord.

Let's walk through each component of The Wheel, beginning at the center with the hub.

Christ the Center

The hub of The Wheel is Jesus Christ. As Dawson Trotman explained it, "If you mean business for God, at the center of your life must be Jesus Christ. . . . From this hub comes your driving power, your guiding power, and your holding power. . . . From Him comes our life, our power to be victorious, and our all-sufficiency."

The act of making Christ central in your life, that is, giving Him the place of true leadership, is an act of your will. There should be a time in your life when you are willing to surrender totally to Christ's authority and lordship.

As you explain the hub to the person you're discipling, look up and discuss together 2 Corinthians 5:17 and Galatians 2:20. These verses describe a life with Christ at the center.

Obedience to Christ

The rim of The Wheel is also part of our response to Christ. It represents our obedience to Him. When you are obedient to Christ and actively following God's leading, it shows in your outward life. People can see the evidences of your faith. The proof of your love for God is your obedience to Him. In fact, none of the spokes of the wheel will hold together unless they are rimmed by this essential element of obedience.

Romans 12:1 and John 14:21 speak to this critical dimension of the Christian life.

The Word

The spoke representing the Word of God is the foundational spoke. In practice, this spoke is perhaps the most crucial element in a balanced Christian life. As God speaks to you through the Scriptures, you can see His principles for life and ministry, learn how to obey, and see Christ as worthy of your unqualified allegiance. When a Christian has a vital personal intake of the Word of God, he is healthy and growing.

If you are helping a new Christian, you can use Joshua 1:8 and 2 Timothy 3:16 to drive home the importance of a strong Word spoke.

Prayer

The other vertical spoke—also representing how we relate to God—is prayer. Prayer should be the natural overflow of meaningful time in the Scriptures. The two go hand in hand. Respond back to God in prayer after He speaks to you through His Word. In this manner, you share your heart with the one who longs for your companionship.

Prayer is how the power of God is unleashed. Personal battles and battles for others are won in prayer, and the cause of Christ is thus furthered. Show the person you are discipling the importance of prayer through verses such as John 15:7 and Philippians 4:6-7.

Fellowship

We now turn to the horizontal elements of The Wheel, representing how we relate with one another. The first horizontal spoke is labeled fellowship.

There is a certain chemistry that takes place as Christians get together to build each other up. This cannot be accomplished if you operate independently and are isolated from other Christians.

To help someone you are discipling grasp how God feels about His children seeking fellowship with each other, look up and discuss Hebrews 10:24-25 and 1 John 1:3.

Witnessing

The final component of The Wheel is the witnessing spoke. The natural overflow of a rich and vibrant life in Christ should be sharing with others how they, too, can have this life. Point a new believer to verses such as Matthew 4:19 and Romans 1:16, so they will see that talking about their faith is an essential part of their new life in Christ.

The Navigators have developed a Bible study and Scripture memory system to help you or someone you are discipling to absorb and apply the principles of The Wheel. The second Bible study book of the "Design for Discipleship Series," called *The Spirit-filled Christian*, contains a Bible study for each element of The Wheel. Series A of the *Topical Memory System* includes each of the verses mentioned above, along with instructions for how to memorize them effectively. These materials are published by NavPress and are available through Christian bookstores or by calling 800-366-7788 (416-499-4615 in Canada).

Adapted from *Growing Strong in God's Family* (NavPress) and *The Navigator* by Robert D. Foster (NavPress, out of print).

The Hand Illustration

Pick up your Bible. How securely can you grasp it with one finger? Silly question. How firm is your hold with two fingers? A child could still pull it away from you. It isn't until you grab your Bible with your whole hand that you get a firm grip.

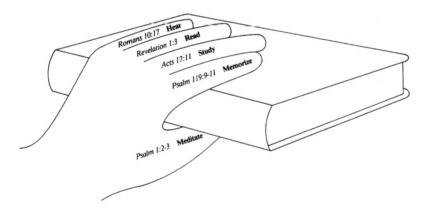

The Hand Illustration is an easy-to-remember tool for showing someone you're discipling how to get a working grasp of the Scriptures. Each finger represents one way to take in the Word of God. A balanced intake of the Bible comes through hearing, reading, studying, and memorizing. Then, as we meditate on the Scriptures during these four activities, they become more personal and specific in helping us grow in Christlikeness.

Let's look in more detail at these five methods of learning from the Bible.

1. Hearing the Word from godly pastors and teachers provides us with insight from Bible study done by others. It also stimulates our appetites for the Scriptures. The weakest finger—the pinkie—represents hearing, because we retain the least through that method of intake (5 percent).

2. Reading gives us an overall picture of the Bible and is also the foundation of the daily quiet time. This activity is represented by the ring finger. We generally retain 15 percent of what we read.

3. Studying the Scriptures deepens our convictions. It requires greater time and effort but results in increased Bible knowledge. Most people retain 35 percent of what they study. This means of intake is represented by the middle finger.

4. Memorizing God's Word enables us to use the Sword of the Spirit to overcome temptations and to have verses readily available for ministering to Christians and nonChristians. Scripture memory stimulates meaningful meditation. The index finger, our strongest finger, represents memorization. We remember 100 percent of what we memorize if we consistently review it.

5. Meditation is the inward process that should accompany each of the other four methods of Scripture intake. This is why meditation is assigned to the thumb. Only the thumb can touch all the other four fingers. By meditating on God's Word as we hear, read, study, and memorize, we discover its transforming power at work in us.

How to Use This Tool

Ask the person you're discipling to trace his hand on a sheet of paper. Have him write the word *hear* on the little finger. Read Romans 10:17 together. On the next finger, have him write the word *read*, then look up Revelation 1:3. The middle finger should be labeled *study*. Read Acts 17:11 together to see an example of men and women who studied the Word of God with dedication. Label the index finger with the word *memorize*, then read Psalm 119:9-11.

Finally, have him write the word *meditate* on the thumb. Look up Psalm 1:2-3 to see the benefits of meditating on the Word. Discuss how meditation can strengthen each of the other four methods for taking in God's Word. Brainstorm ways to increase your intake of Scripture during the next month.

Adapted from *The 2:7 Series, Course Four* (NavPress)

TRY STUDYING THE BIBLE IN A NEW WAY.

Capture the joy of Bible study. This handbook, compiled from the pages of *Discipleship Journal* magazine, offers creative ways to delight in and learn from Scripture. From word studies to role-playing to personal reflection, both clergy and laypeople explain how to infuse study with fresh insight — and without compromising the Bible's meaning, integrity, or reliability.
Discipleship Journal's Best Bible Study Methods

by Discipleship Journal
1-57683-291-0

To get your copies, visit your local bookstore, call 1-800-366-7788, or log on to www.navpress.com. Ask for a FREE catalog of NavPress products. Offer 6405.

NAVPRESS ®
BRINGING TRUTH TO LIFE
www.navpress.com

LOOKING FOR YOUR NEXT BIBLE STUDY?

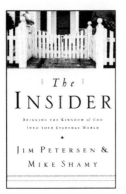
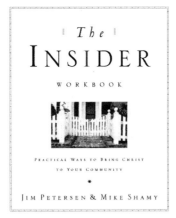

A DISCIPLING GUIDE ANYONE CAN USE.

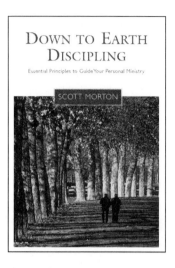

Here's a practical, friendly guide to everything you need to know about one-to-one discipling without terrifying you or those you want to reach. It divides the process into simple, manageable steps, based firmly on biblical principles.

Down-to-Earth Discipling
by Scott Morton
1-57683-339-9

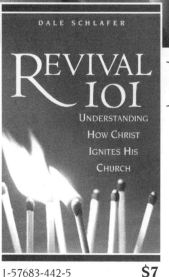